AF479786

7 CHAKRAS
IN 7 DAYS

ERIN DINSMORE

Aberdeen Books

Ashland, Oregon

Library of Congress Catalog Number: 20-22911882

ISBN (Paperback): 979-8-3485-8638-6

Third Edition

February 20th, 2025

First Edition

November 11th, 2024

THE 7 CHAKRAS OF SELF

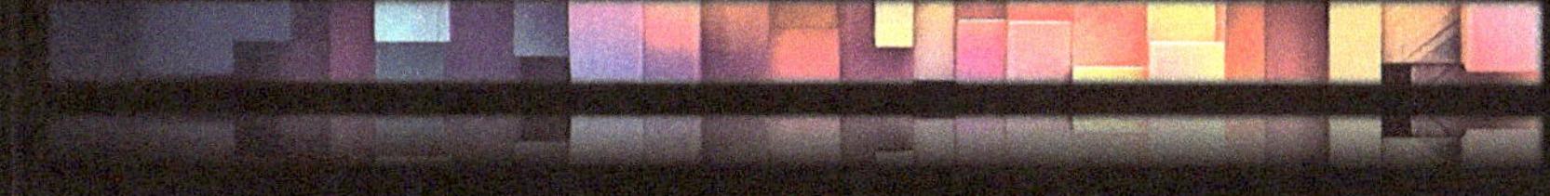

How aware are we of our own bodies? I remember looking down at my arm once after I'd cut it, thinking, *'I have no idea how to grow new skin or heal this wound. My body knows how to do it, and I don't? That must mean my body knows more about itself than I do.'* This simple observation sparked a deeper question: How much do we truly know about our **energy body**, the unseen force that influences nearly every aspect of our lives?

What if the key to unlocking your fullest potential, to healing emotional wounds, and to living a truly vibrant life—was hidden within a secret energy system you never knew you had? Feeling anxious or insecure? That's your root chakra, your foundation, calling for attention. Struggling to express your authentic self? Your throat chakra might be blocked. Feeling creatively stifled or disconnected from your passions? Your sacral chakra needs a little love. We've become so focused on our outward identity, our achievements, and possessions, that we've lost touch with our inner world, the wisdom of our bodies and the depths of our souls. We strive to grow our bank accounts, but what about growing our awareness? What if the key to unlocking our fullest potential, healing our emotional wounds, and living a truly vibrant life—lies within a secret energy system we never knew we had?

This is where the chakras come in. These spinning wheels of light, mapped along our spine, are not just ancient spiritual myths, they are as real as your arms and legs, and they hold the keys to unlocking our innate power, healing old patterns, and creating a life that truly reflects our soul's purpose. The chakras are a map to your inner landscape, a guide to understanding the intricate connection between your energy body and your everyday experiences. You chakras hold the key to unlocking your innate power to align with a life that truly reflects your soul's purpose.

But here's where it gets even more profound. The chakras aren't just about managing your outer world; they hold within them divine concepts, universal laws that can help you evolve and understand what keeps you stuck in life. As you delve into each chakra, you're not just gaining knowledge; you're unlocking ancestral wisdom, activating dormant potential, and stepping onto a path of deep personal and spiritual growth. For thousands of years, yogis and mystics have worked with the chakras to achieve higher states of consciousness, to heal physical ailments, and to manifest their deepest desires. These swirling vortexes of energy, mapped along your spine, correlate to specific organs, emotions, and even stages of spiritual development. They're a profound testament to the interconnectedness of your being, a reminder that you are more than just a physical body. You are a being of light, of energy, and it's time to unravel your inner self.

———

A wonderful system to integrate the 7 chakras into your life is to fold them into the 7 days of the week. For this, we start on Monday with your roots on Earth and work our way to Sunday where we spend time in the Soul Mind in the stars. The chakras are probably the most important aspects of your life and have everything to do with what you do, who you are, and how you feel. These spinning balls of energy act as the supercomputers of your soul. They each carry abilities and secrets, and they all have a direct impact on your life, well-being, and what you are able to create in this reality. This is the path to heal your past and awaken beyond the mind of limitation.

The whispers of your soul echo in the chambers of your chakras; listen deeply, and find the healing you have always carried within.

A quick note: Remember, the true power of the chakras lies not in stories or symbols, but within your own experience. Detach from the past. The number of flower petals, the names, the shapes, the structures—these were guides at the time, not rigid truths—and they can transform with new awareness into the now. Let go of the need to be right and allow your mind to expand. Allow yourself to feel your way through it and trust your inner wisdom. These are your chakras and they are yours to discover, to explore, and unfold. There is nothing to compare. Enjoy the journey into self. Let go of the mind and surrender to the wisdom of your heart and soul. Today, we bring these sacred ancestral tools into the now.

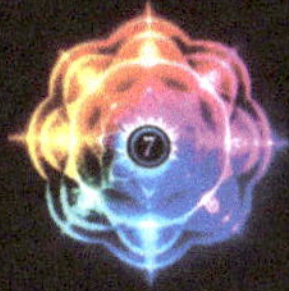

As you walk through each day, you will find three paths. The path of Ego Realization, The path of Sound and Frequency, and The Path of Universal Knowledge. Mind, Body, and Spirit. Here are some important overviews of the journey ahead:

The Ego & The Self (Mind)

Each chakra gives us a deeper look at how we can start to identify this inner landscape and how it relates to our inward and outward identity. The ego acts as "the mind of self". A belief that we are an individual and that our outward identities are the reality. Through this system we will find the sensual identity as it relates to out soul. We have an inward and outward identity and each day we can unravel a little more of our inner truth.

Sound & Frequency (Body)

As Nikola Tesla wisely said,

"If you want to find the secrets of the universe, think in terms of energy, frequency, and vibration."

Each chakra responds to a very specific frequency. These frequencies open a pathway to deeper levels of healing and release by harmonizing your energy centers, even without your mind consciously understanding the process. You can use these tones to heal specific blocks and wounds, as well as to experience your inward and outward self, the aspects of "doing" and "being".

The 7 Divine Laws Of The Universe (Soul)

When reaching back into the ancient Vedas and ancestral knowledge, you see a slew of tools we left along the way. One of the most powerful aspects of our chakras are the divine concepts dwelling within. Knowledge in its most potent form.

Our lives and our universe operate according to a set of fundamental principles – *the seven divine laws.* These laws are not rigid dictates but rather a harmonious symphony of energy, a sacred geometry that shapes all of creation. Imagine these laws as a unified whole, a single divine truth, broken into seven distinct facets so that we, as humans, can grasp their essence and apply them to our lives. To awaken.

These laws are reflected within us, in the intricate system of energy centers we call *chakras.* Each chakra corresponds to a specific law, offering a pathway to self-discovery and healing. By understanding and embodying these laws, we can evolve and align with the universal flow of energy and create a life of purpose and alignment. Each day we will integrate each chakra with their corresponding universal truth. These laws, when understood and applied, can be powerful tools for personal growth, healing, and spiritual awakening.

The journey within.

"The chakras are the meeting places of the physical and subtle energetic bodies.

By understanding the chakras, we can begin to comprehend the totality of our

being and learn to work with our bodies as instruments of spiritual awakening."

Pg. — 65 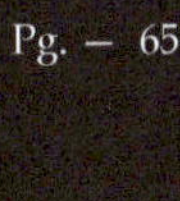 **SUNDAY** - Crown Chakra
Sahasrara

Pg. — 53  **SATURDAY** - 3rd Eye Chakra
Ajna

Pg. — 41  **FRIDAY** - Throat Chakra
Vishuddha

Pg. — 31  **THURSDAY** - Heart Chakra
Anahata

Pg. — 21  **WEDNESDAY** - Solar Plexus
Manipura

Pg. — 11  **TUESDAY** - Sacral Chakra
Svadhisthana

Pg. — 01  **MONDAY** - Root Chakra
Muladhara

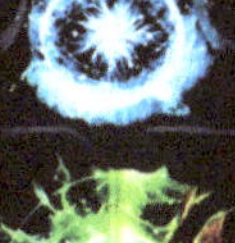

Affirmation

"I am safe, I am secure, I am grounded in the Earth."

Day 1
Root Chakra

Muladhara – "I Am"

Your Foundation on Earth.

Your root chakra is a vibrant red ball of spinning light, pulsating with the Earth's energy. Feel the crimson red energy churning at the base of your spine. The home of your Kundalini energy from the Tree of Life. Today is all about creation, surrender, and abundance. In practice, all you need to do today is ground yourself in the Earth and focus your attention on being with nature. Just wake up, go outside, and stand barefoot on the grass. Feel your powerful root beneath the surface, our foundation. It governs survival, security, and primal energy. On an emotional level, it houses instincts, fear, and the desire for groundedness. It's your anchor, your foundation, your connection to the physical world. As you nurture this chakra, you'll feel a deeper sense of belonging, stability, and security in your body and in the world.

"I AM"

The Seed of Your Existence

More than just survival, the root chakra is about embodying your "I Am" presence. "I am. I exist. I belong." These are the fundamental affirmations of the root chakra. It's about recognizing your inherent right to exist, to take up space, and to feel safe and secure in your body and in the world.

This can be a challenge for many, especially those who have experienced trauma or disconnection from their bodies. That part of us that is afraid of life, afraid of death, afraid of the Earth. We can feel ungrounded, anxious, or disconnected from our physical selves, but the root chakra reminds us that we are rooted in the Earth, that we belong here, and that we are safe—even in darkness, we her, we are grounded and protected.

"Muladhara"

The name "Muladhara" comes from Sanskrit, with "Mula" meaning "root" and "adhara" meaning "support" or "base." This reflects the chakra's role as our energetic foundation, connecting us to the Earth and providing stability and security. The Sanskrit shape has 4 petals to represent the four directions for grounding.

The Muladhara chakra is located at the base of the spine and is our center of creation and survival. It's associated with our basic needs, our sense of security, and our connection to the physical world. When balanced, Muladhara provides a sense of stability, safety, and belonging. It allows us to feel grounded, centered, and connected to our physical bodies and the Earth.

The Ego's Influence (Mind)

The Ego is the Mind of Self so we always check in with the choice between expressing from our rational mind or the heart mind. In terms of ego, the wounded root craves control and material stability. Remember that the ego can sometimes influence any chakra, including the root chakra. This triggers our energetic house of survival causing our sense of security to become dependent on external factors, such as possessions, relationships, or social status. We might find ourselves driven by fear of scarcity or a need to control our environment, which can inadvertently reinforce these patterns of separation in our lives.

Instead of being led by the ego's tendencies, consider exploring grounding from a place of inner strength and connection to the Earth. You cultivate a sense of belonging and security that arises from within, independent of external circumstances. Today, you can embrace the present moment and trust in the universe's support, allowing yourself to feel safe and grounded in the here and now.

SOUND & FREQUENCY (Body)

Healing Frequency - 396 Hz

The frequency 396 Hz is associated with the root chakra to:

- o Ground and Stabilize: It helps to ground your energy and create a sense of stability and security.

- o Release Fear and Guilt: This frequency is also associated with releasing fear, anxiety, and guilt, which can block the root chakra.

- o Promote Transformation: Some believe 396 Hz can help to transform negative emotions and limiting beliefs, paving the way for personal growth and transformation.

"Lam"

"Lam" is the seed mantra or bija mantra associated with Muladhara. Chanting "Lam" helps to:

- **Activate and Balance the Chakra:** It vibrates within the lower abdomen, stimulating and harmonizing the energy of Muladhara.

- **Enhance Grounding:** It helps to strengthen your connection to the Earth and promote a sense of stability and security.

- **Release Fear:** Chanting "Lam" 33 times in quick rhythmic loops can help to release fear, anxiety, and other negative emotions that stem from survival.

Divine Law Of The Universe (Soul)

GENERATION

This journey through the chakras and the seven divine laws is a cyclical dance between the soul and the self, a roadmap for identifying your outward and inward identity. By understanding these laws in relation to the dual nature of our minds, we begin to shed the limitations of the ego-mind by embracing the boundless wisdom of the higher mind. This is a path of integration, of wholeness, of recognizing the divine spark within and aligning with the universal flow of creation. By studying and becoming these divine agreements, you can awaken to your true nature as an infinite being, capable of manifesting a life of purpose, joy, and fulfillment.

Gender/Generation (Root Chakra): The ego-mind often seeks security and validation through external sources, leading to a sense of lack and instability. The Law of Gender/Generation highlights the creative power of the universe and the interplay of masculine and feminine energies within us. By grounding ourselves in the root chakra and embracing our creative potential, we can cultivate a sense of inner security and contribute to the ongoing process of growth and evolution.

What is the Universal Law of Generation, and how is it associated with the root?

The Universal Law of 'Generation' or the 7th Divine Concept within the 1st Chakra, states that everything in the universe is energy, and this energy can be manifested into physical form through our root chakra. Generation means, TO CREATE! The root chakra, as our foundation and connection to the Earth, plays a key role in this manifestation process.

o **Grounding and Creation:** The Law of Generation teaches us that by grounding our energy and aligning our thoughts and emotions with our desires, we can manifest our dreams into reality. The root chakra, when balanced, provides the stability and security needed to manifest our energy for creation.

o Abundance and Prosperity: The root chakra is also associated with abundance and prosperity. When we feel safe and secure, we are more likely to attract abundance into our lives. By releasing fear of lack and embracing a mindset of abundance, we can create a fertile ground for manifesting our desires.

Divine Guide - Veer N'Ka'A (Ancestral)
The Crimson Dragon

From the heart of the Earth emerges Veer N'Ka'A, the Red Dragon, its scales shimmering like rubies. This magnificent creature embodies the primal forces of grounding, security, and survival, but it lives in the divinity of our Earth mother. Veer N'Ka'A sees Gaia as the mother of us all. With a loving Lam that reverberates through your very bones, Veer N'Ka'A awakens your connection to the Earth, reminding you of your inherent unity. This dragon's love is wise, powerful, and protective, a fiery embrace that encourages you to connect to the lower realms of this divine planet.

'It's rare that a child has a parent with a deeply established root chakra who can model that chakra so their child can naturally develop a healthy and vibrant foundation. I am here to be a guiding light that your root chakra can feel to help it see itself. Your root chakra is where the body forms it's connection to the Earth. The root chakra also allows for the releasing and integration of ancestral energy. Your crown chakra will connect you to the masculine spirit above, the root connects you to the feminine material spirit below. Most human beings are not connected energetically with the heart of this living world. I am here to be a type of warmth to make it easier for your roots to connect into Gaia's heart, to reconnect, to help you feel like you belong and to help you feel safe. We invite you all into the Great Return."

Activity For The Day

Today is a perfect day for a walking meditation. Get that body moving into the week ahead. A walking mediation is simply to step slowly and mindfully out in nature and with one foot you say, "I am" and with the other you say, "Gai." or "Earth." Try to spend at least 30 minutes in this grounding space. Move slowly, breathe deeply, and connect to your root energy down into the heart of the Earth.

Yoga Pose

Mountain Pose (Tadasana). This is the perfect starting place for Day 1. This pose helps you find your standing center, it can be done anywhere at any time and it activates your root while seeking total balance in the rest of your body.

The Path To Unconditional Love

The root chakra begins our journey of separation. It holds 6 parts conditional 1 part unconditional. You can see this in geometry as the x and y axis. Our journey to unfold follows the geometric expansion from conditional love (structure and limitation) to unconditional love (transcendence of the conditional world of limitation.) This is a great chakra to see conditional and unconditional as judgment and love. This chakra then begins with 6 parts judgment 1 part love. (Judgment is a form of separation.)

"I am. I exist. I belong"

Affirmation

"I am sensual, I am free, I am what I am what I am."

Day 2
Sacral Chakra

Svadhisthana – "I feel"

Your Sensual Identity.

Turn on the music, 417hz, and let your sacral wake up to the sound of your deepest identity. The *"I am"* in us all becomes curated into a *Self.* Ask yourself this: **Who am I? How did I form this identity? Does my outward expression of who I am match how I feel on the inside?** Your second chakra is all about **identity** and **sexuality,** and today we are embracing both your positive and negative aspects while learning how to integrate them both into your authentic expression of self.

Put your right hand just below the belly button and feel your sacred sacral center. This giant pulsating ball of orange energy spinning and churning. Within the Sacral realm lies **sensuality, pleasure, and creativity.** It governs emotions like joy, passion, and the desire for connection. When it's blocked or out of balance, **it seeks self-gratification and validation**. Today is all about exploring your relationship with your identity and being exactly who you are from the inside out. Your sacral chakra is a radiant orange ball of spinning light, pulsating with creative energy and emotional expression. It's your source of joy, passion, and connection. *As you nurture this chakra, you'll feel a deeper sense of aliveness, creativity, and emotional well-being.*

Forming Your Authentic Identity

More than just pleasure, the sacral chakra is about honoring your emotions. ***"I feel. I flow. I create."*** These are the expressions of the sacral chakra. It's about recognizing and accepting the full spectrum of your emotions, allowing them to flow freely up into your solar plexus without judgment or suppression. This can be a challenge for many, especially those who have been taught to suppress their emotions or who have experienced emotional trauma. We may feel numb, disconnected, or overwhelmed by our emotions. But the sacral chakra reminds us that our emotions are a source of wisdom and guidance, a vital part of our human experience. Speak to your chakra and just try saying, ***"Thank you. I see you, and I love you."***

Rest your hand on your lower abdomen and let it purge what you were, your old stories, and release it all to become something new. You hold sexual identity here as well so it's a great day to heal your sexual past. You can start by remembering that we all carry some sexual shrapnel in our 2nd, so today we rest our hand on our sacral and thank it for all it has endured. We then remember, this is actually the house of sensuality, so we can take a moment today to transform our own perceptions of sexuality back into a more sensual state of our expression.

"Svadhisthana"

The name *"Svadhisthana"* comes from Sanskrit and means "one's own abode" or "dwelling place of the self." This reflects the chakra's association with our sense of identity, our emotions, and our creative expression. **It's associated with our relationships, our sexuality, and our ability to experience joy and abundance.** The ancient shape has 6 petals, the number 6 mirroring the six senses, duality, and union of opposites. When balanced, Swadhisthana allows us to *embrace our emotions, express ourselves creatively, and connect with others in healthy and fulfilling ways.* Picture two opposing magnets inside your belly with a little silver marble in between–that is you. Life pulls you between both magnets, rolling back and forth, up and down. Positive and negative and everything in between. This represents the push and pull of your identity which is also housed in this chakra. Today, your identity is a fresh slab of clay on your potter's wheel. Simply carve off what no longer serves you and pay attention to this area today to let it define who you really are in the now. **Sacral Day** is all about understanding *polarity* and spending time with your identity. If you find yourself feeling, "That's not who I am" then, *tell them who you are.* Express your soul today!

The Ego's Influence on Emotional Flow (Mind)

Remember that the ego can sometimes influence any chakra, including the sacral chakra. When this happens, our emotional expression may become blocked or distorted. We might find ourselves seeking external validation for our creativity or using pleasure as a means of escape or control. *Authentic expression is born right here, not in the mind.* Instead of being led by the ego's tendencies, *consider exploring your sacral chakra from a place of self-acceptance and authenticity.* Explore new ways of expressing yourself. You could allow your emotions to flow freely, expressing them in healthy and creative ways. You could embrace your sensuality and connect with others from a place of genuine intimacy and vulnerability. Just make a new choice today and see how the shoes fit.

Healing Frequency – 417 Hz

- **Promote Emotional Healing:** It helps to release emotional blockages and facilitate healing from past traumas by releasing stagnant energy in the body.

- **Enhance Creativity:** This frequency is also associated with creativity, passion, and self-expression. Feel your sexuality stir within, *then use it to create.*

- **Facilitate Change:** The 417 Hz frequency can help to break negative patterns and create positive change in your life by restabilizing your energy field.

BIJA MANTRA

"Vam"

"Vam" is the seed mantra or bija mantra associated with Swadhisthana. Chanting "Vam" in 33 short repetitive sounds will open the chakra energy to:

- **Activate and Balance the Chakra:** It vibrates within the lower abdomen, stimulating and harmonizing the energy of Swadhisthana.

- **Enhance Creativity:** It helps to unlock your creative potential and express yourself authentically.

- **Promote Emotional Flow:** Chanting "Vam" can help to release emotional blockages and promote a healthy flow of emotions.

Divine Law Of The Universe (Soul)

POLARITY

This journey through the chakras and the seven divine laws is a cyclical dance between the soul and the self, a roadmap for identifying your outward and inward identity. By understanding these laws in relation to the dual nature of our minds, we begin to shed the limitations of the ego-mind by embracing the boundless wisdom of the higher mind. This is a path of integration, of wholeness, of recognizing the divine spark within and aligning with the universal flow of creation. By studying and becoming these divine agreements, you can awaken to your true nature as an infinite being, capable of manifesting a life of purpose, joy, and fulfillment.

Polarity (Sacral Chakra): The ego-mind often tries to present a perfect, idealized version of ourselves to the world, suppressing or denying aspects that we deem unacceptable. The 6th Law of Polarity recognizes the duality inherent in all things, encouraging us to embrace both our light and shadow aspects. By connecting with the sacral chakra and integrating our polarities, we can achieve greater wholeness and authenticity. This is where our authentic self is born, in the fluidity and dynamism of embracing both polarities, like the sun and the moon held in balance, you are always both.

What is the Universal Law of Polarity, and how is it associated with the sacral?

The Universal Law of Polarity, or the Divine Concept within the 2nd Chakra, states that everything in the universe has an opposite but interconnected aspect. Meaning, so do you. This includes masculine and feminine energies, light and shadow, and joy and sorrow. I see this as a beautiful little silver ball inside your sacral, the house of identity. It rolls between these two magnets always changing, *polarity*, always becoming something new, *identity*, and always expressing it, *sensuality*. Polarity is to say that you will always have someone pulling you from left to right and your goal is to learn how to stand in center *by becoming aware of your inner truth.*

o **Embracing Duality:** The Law of Polarity teaches us that by embracing and integrating the dualities within ourselves and the world around us, we can create balance and harmony. The sacral chakra, when balanced, allows us to experience the full spectrum of emotions and integrate them into our creative expression.

o **Creative Flow:** The sacral chakra is also associated with the creative flow of the universe. By embracing the dance of polarities, we can tap into this creative energy and manifest our desires.

Divine Guide – Ur'Than'Ran (Ancestral)

The "Terracotta" Dragon

From the flowing waters of emotion emerges **Ur'Than'Ran**, the Terracotta Dragon, its scales shimmering with the colors of the last sunset. This graceful creature embodies the creative forces of **passion, pleasure, and self-expression**. With a loving dance that ignites your inner fire, **Ur'Than'Ran** awakens your connection to the sacral chakra, reminding you of your innate capacity for joy and abundance. This dragon's love is sensual and playful, an invitation to embrace your emotions and express the unique rhythm of your soul.

"Your root chakra goes directly down into the center of the Earth, but your sacral roots are just below the surface reaching out. When not in touch, it's like an orphaned child. It will feel lost and alone and that will create various problems. Lack of joy and pleasure, and enjoyment in life. A lack of a deep sense of

groundedness and ease, of comfort, of homeliness. But when that chakra starts to become aligned with its divine counterpart, the chakra that matches the whole body of the cosmos, then it can rest in a state of peace. When it's being supported it starts to mirror the qualities of your divine counterpart."

Activity For The Day

Today is all about observing your relationship with *your identity* and learning how to transform.

- Delete The Past: We present ourselves to the world and then we need to live up to it. Your past is staring at you every day. If you are feeling courageous about transformation, then today you can choose one social media account, go one year back or all the way, **and delete it all** (or Archive it). Then post a meme that says, "I thank the past for what I have learned but today I start anew. Happy Sacral Chakra Day." You are saying, *"I have transformed my past and released it because I learned from it and expanded."* Welcome to the Now. Naked and undefined.

Yoga Pose

Crescent Moon Pose (Anjaneyasana)—Open your hips and tap into your sensual flow.

Svadhisthana

CHAKRA ELEMENTS

417 hz   "I FEEL"   'Vam'

Gland/Body Part: Gonads (ovaries/testes), lower abdomen, kidneys, bladder

Stones: Carnelian, Moonstone, Orange Calcite

Smells: Ylang-Ylang, Sandalwood, Citrus

Colors: Orange, Peach, Terracotta

Foods for Today: Fruits, Nuts, Seeds, Chocolate

Sacred Geometry: The Crescent Moon shape is the connection to lunar energy, emotions, and the subconscious

Principle— Creative Reproduction Of Being

Element - Water

Polarity

"I feel. I flow. I create."

"Through my truth, I find my soul fire."

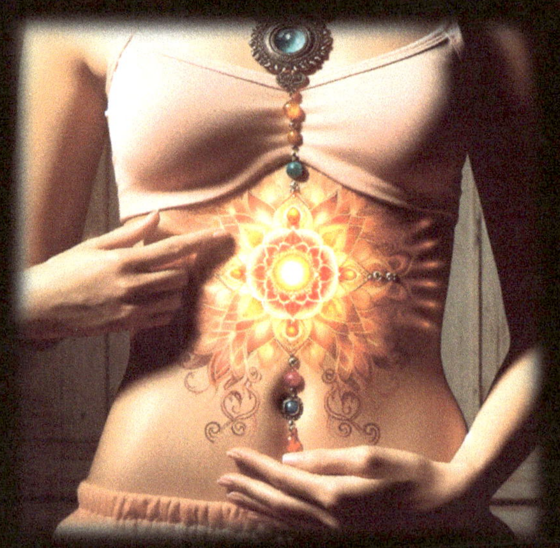

Day 3
Solar Plexus Chakra

Manipura – "I Do"

Your Inner Fire.

Feel the warm yellow energy swirling in your solar plexus just above your belly button, your inner sun. It's your center of willpower, self-esteem, and confidence, radiating like a golden beacon. Today, stand tall and proud. This is *accountability day*. Learning to be emotionally honest with yourself for your actions–your *cause and effect* with the world. ***Honesty fuels the fire within. Accountability unlocks the gates.*** Try to be internally honest all day today. You are always making choices and those choices have energy that effects everyone around you regardless of what you are thinking, Be mindful of the way you treat others and how it makes you feel. Lying here keeps you stuck.

This is where we bring relentless honesty back into our lives. Not to be morally just, but inner honesty is how you start to feel your heart signals again. This accountability of *self* releases the blocks and anxiety from this powerful emotional center in your upper abdomen. Try to embrace the *Triangle of Truth*, do **your words** match **your actions**, and do **your actions** match **your thoughts**? For most of us, the answer is no. ***We say one thing, do another, and think something else.*** Today is all about unfolding the blocks from your current identity you created from a mind of fear and survival because that mind is not allowing your soul to co-create who you really are. Today is about one question and one question only: ***How can you*** *decide who you are if you've already decided?* Your mind created a carefully curated version of 'you' but now it's time to learn your inner truth, the soul that drives it all, and become something new.

Your solar plexus chakra is a radiant yellow ball of spinning light, pulsating with willpower and transformative energy but it needs your authentic voice to truly shine. It's your source of personal power, self-esteem, and the ability to create positive change. *As you nurture this chakra with your new awareness, you'll feel a deeper sense of confidence, purpose, and determination.*

"I DO"

Your Fire Of Truth

More than just willpower, the solar plexus chakra is about taking action and manifesting your desires. ***"I do. I act. I transform."*** *All without the constraints of the mind.* ***That is how you find your truth.*** These are the unblocked declarations of the solar plexus chakra. It's about recognizing your inner strength, setting clear intentions, and taking decisive action to heal and release the wounds that block your inner expression. This chakra holds an incredible challenge, to live in a rational identity which crates anxiety and blocks in your solar plexus, or to remove the idea of self and learn how to express with fearless abandon. *"This is who I am now."*

This can be a challenge for many, especially those who have experienced setbacks or self-doubt. We may feel powerless, indecisive, or afraid to show the world who we really are. But the solar plexus chakra reminds us that we have the inner fire to transform our fear of expression, to overcome self-judgment, to remove blame, *and to finally see that it is in our flaws that we find ourselves.* The flaws are what make you so unique, so why are we so afraid to show them to the world? *This is also who you are.*

"Manipura"

The name *"Manipura"* comes from Sanskrit and means "city of jewels" or "lustrous gem." This reflects the chakra's association with our inner fire, our willpower, and our sense of personal power. Manipura, the third chakra, is located in the solar plexus, the area between your navel and rib cage. When balanced, Manipura empowers us to step into our personal power, pursue our goals with authentic confidence, and create positive change in our lives.

The Ego's Influence On Your Expression (Mind)

Today we study the sacred concept of *transparency*. The authentic expression of our abilities and flaws without judgment. This beautiful yellow powerhouse is the energetic generator of experience. To know you have processed the Fifth Truth you would be free of blame. This is a surrender to **accountability**. A deflection of accountability is to say, "It wasn't me," which *creates a wall of resistance to your truth.* Free yourself of all blame because today is about surrendering, as you say, *"I am responsible for all of this."* Your mind wants to defend you at all costs and today is about grabbing that captain's wheel and taking ownership of this world and everyone in it. No more waiting for others to act, no more stories to keep you safe, you step right into the cause and effect of this world and learn to engage, take charge, and commit to who you are.

Remember that the 'mind of self' can influence any chakra. This exact chakra holds the wall between your ego and your authentic self. An energetic valve that opens and closes based on your inner truth. When this chakra is blocked, *our willpower may become distorted by the ego's need for control, dominance, or self-aggrandizement.* We might find ourselves *driven by a need to prove ourselves or to dominate others,* which can create conflict and hinder our personal growth. Instead of being led by the ego's tendencies, consider exploring your solar plexus chakra *from a place of self-awareness and authenticity. You can use your power to serve your fear-based mind or unfold it to allow your most authentic expression to rule your creations.* Try to transform your willpower to create positive change, to empower yourself and others, and to align with your soul's purpose.

SOUND & FREQUENCY (Body)

Healing Frequency – 528 Hz

The frequency 528 Hz is associated with the solar plexus chakra and activates to:

- **Promote Transformation and Healing:** It helps to transform negative energy and promote physical and emotional healing.

- **Enhance Self-Esteem:** This frequency is also associated with self-esteem, confidence, and personal power.

- **Manifest Miracles:** 528 Hz can help to manifest miracles and create positive change in your life. Dream away but dream from the heart and soul—not the head.

BIJA MANTRA

"Ram"

"Ram" is the seed mantra or bija mantra associated with Manipura. Chanting "Ram" in 33 short repetitive sounds will open the chakra energy to:

o **Activate and Balance the Chakra:** It vibrates within the solar plexus, stimulating and harmonizing the energy of Manipura.

o **Enhance Willpower:** It helps to strengthen your willpower, self-discipline, and determination.

o **Promote Transformation**: Chanting "Ram" over and over again can transform fear and self-doubt into courage and confidence. If you feel anxious, speak Ram!

Divine Law Of The Universe (Soul)

CAUSE & EFFECT

Cause and effect (Solar Plexus): The ego may believe it is acting freely, but often it is the result of habits and conditioning. This creates a feedback loop of unintended results. The Law of Cause and Effect encourages us to become aware of our motivations. By cultivating a strong and balanced solar plexus, we take ownership of ourselves, become conscious, and create from that point, which is the best place of manifestation.

What is the Universal Law of Cause and Effect, and how is it associated with the Solar Plexus?

The Universal Law of Cause and Effect, or the *5th* Divine Concept within the 3rd Chakra, states that every action generates an energy, a force of reaction, that returns to us in kind. Like a boomerang, our thoughts, words, and deeds ripple outwards, shaping our reality and inevitably circling back to us. The Solar Plexus, the fiery center of personal power and will, is where we ignite these causes, and therefore, experience their effects. It is represented by a bright spinning golden gear. with every action or thought, it spins, sending out the request and receiving back a manifestation of that request.

- **Empowered Action:** The Law of Cause and Effect reminds us that we are not passive recipients of fate, but active creators of our experience. When the Solar Plexus is balanced, we take responsibility for our actions, understanding that we hold the power to shape our lives through conscious choices. We become mindful of the energy we put out, knowing it will return.

- **Karma and Consequence:** The Solar Plexus is deeply tied to the concept of karma – not as punishment, but as the natural consequence of our actions. A balanced Solar Plexus allows us to learn from past experiences, understand the effects of our choices, and consciously choose actions that align with our desired outcomes. We move from reactivity to proactivity.

- **Will and Manifestation:** The Solar Plexus is the seat of our willpower. The Law of Cause and Effect demonstrates that focused intention, fueled by a strong Solar Plexus, is a potent force for manifestation. When we align our will with positive, constructive causes, we attract positive, constructive effects into our lives.

Divine Guide - Taixuan 太玄 *(Tay-Shuen)* (Ancestral)

The Golden Dragon

From the radiant sun within your being emerges *Taixuan*, the Golden Dragon, her angelic body gleaming like an angel made of treasure. She is the Goddess of pleasure and creation, and she is very adamant that she is not yellow, she is very much gold. **This majestic creature embodies your willpower, soul expression, and your challenges in Ego.** With a playful twist, she ignites your inner child, *Taixuan* awakens your connection to the solar plexus chakra, reminding you of your innate ability to leave the Self and find your inner playful energy. She is here to help you manifest your sacred desires—but don't distract her with 'wants' and ego treats. Her love is infectious and inspiring, a golden light that guides you towards fulfilling your soul's purpose. **The is the place we find our blocks between the unmanifested and manifested worlds.** There is a mystery that unites these two realms, and the original name for this unknown place is, *Xuan*. **"The mystery of mysteries."**

'For those of you who are interested in astrology, my primary sign would be Leo. That can give you in indication of my energy. I am a vibrant, playful being. Very childlike and freeing. My words are not important for it's the energy I am bringing in, the knowing. To know. I am not here to give you intellectual knowledge that your mind can dissect and analyze, I am here to give you your knowledge back. I want to return to you what has always been yours. So many of you are struggling with the ups and downs of life, and the main reason for that is a lack of knowledge. Not intellectual understanding—but self-knowledge, spiritual knowledge, mystical knowledge, knowledge of the supreme mystery. The solar plexus is connected to your sense of identity and healthy self-esteem. Where you shine like the sun. Where you know who you are, your purpose in this life. Shame often constricts you here. There is confusion because you are taught that you aren't supposed to be the way that you are. You radiate yourself out to the world with joy. You do not see yourself as in superior or inferior to others, you simply are who you are and you know who you are meant to be—and you shine."

Activity For The Day

Today is about learning how to unblock your abdominal expressions by removing the control of the mind. So we remember how to integrate into the now and look for new ways to engage with the energy around us.

- *Grab a notebook and pen. Write down two sections; "Inner" and 'Outer' with 1-5 numbers for each. Spend 1 hour timed in silence walking around your house. Find 5 things that seem neglected or broken, and 5 places you could improve or create something new in your home. Redesign, add some new paint, whatever your creative heart desires.*

- *Now spend 1 timed hour outside on the property around you. Again, spend time in stillness observing what you may have never noticed. Write down 5 things that seem neglected or broken and 5 things that you could create and transform.*

- *Stop. Don't read this until you're done. Now, pick 1 neglected item from your inner home, and 1 neglected item from your outer world, and go fix it. Use Google, whatever you need, and learn how to fix it yourself. Then pick one item from your inner to create and transform into something new and then do the same with 1 item from your outer list. Renovate, create, transform.*

*The goal is to remember that your energy is interacting with everything around you. To see that we can become so entrenched in our minds that our energetic expression is often dimmed because we are not in a state of accountability with the world around us. Our wounds cause us to hide and buy our way around truly being engaged. **Today is about taking responsibility for everything.** This is your world, you are a co-creator, and it's time to commit and engage back into the now.*

Yoga Pose

Boat Pose (Navasana)—Build core strength and radiate your confident sunshine.

Honesty fuels the fire within. Accountability unlocks the gates. Opening the

solar plexus is how you become the master of your destiny.

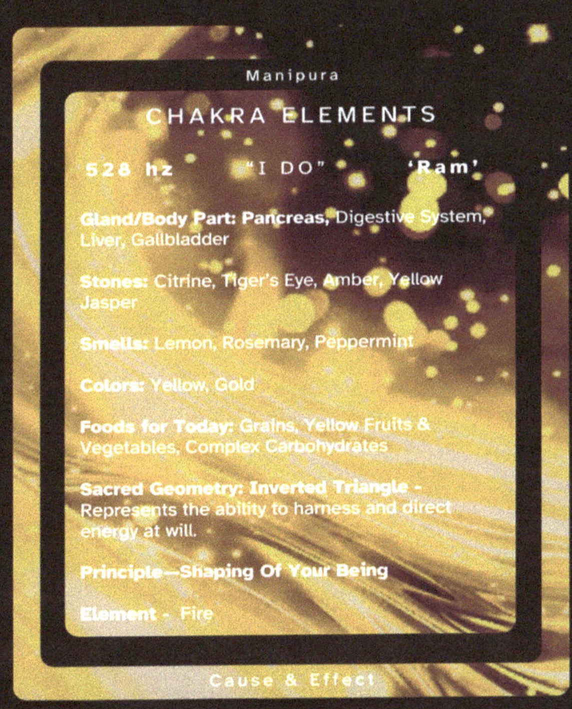
Manipura

CHAKRA ELEMENTS

528 hz   "I DO"   'Ram'

Gland/Body Part: Pancreas, Digestive System, Liver, Gallbladder

Stones: Citrine, Tiger's Eye, Amber, Yellow Jasper

Smells: Lemon, Rosemary, Peppermint

Colors: Yellow, Gold

Foods for Today: Grains, Yellow Fruits & Vegetables, Complex Carbohydrates

Sacred Geometry: Inverted Triangle - Represents the ability to harness and direct energy at will.

Principle—Shaping Of Your Being

Element - Fire

Cause & Effect

"I am. I feel. I express."

Affirmation

"I am sensual, I am free, I am, what I am, what I am."

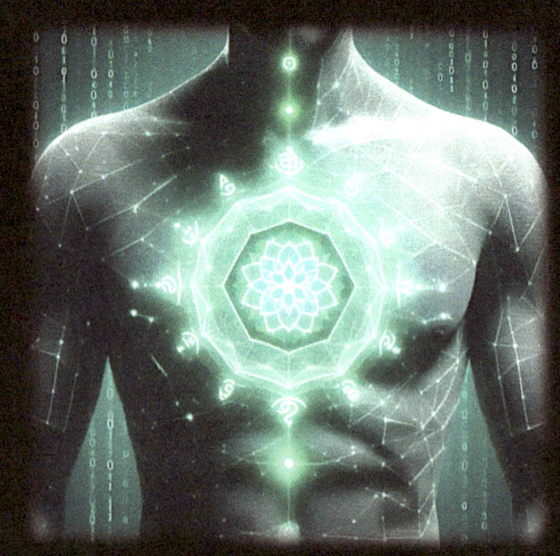

Day 4
Heart Chakra

Anahata – "I Love"

The House Of Harmony.

Rest your right hand on the center of your chest. Feel this incredible chakra stir itself awake. This is where your physical and spiritual energy meet. If God was an electric plug, this is where he plugs in. This is where you connect to the electric currents of source itself. This is the love of the universe.

Ask yourself this question while you open the Heart Chakra today: What does *unconditional* love mean to you? Does it come from your husband or wife? Friends or family? Well, those all have contracts and conditions. Our children get love for good grades or a clean room, our friends get love when we feel loved in return. We hoard our love because we forgot that we are made of it. We can see how our love has become conditional which causes the mind to seek validation and promises of love in return.

Heart Chakra Day allows us to remember that we can access our own limitless love from within. Feel it now. Feel it stir within you in this powerful kingdom. The Heart Chakra is the house of *unconditional love, compassion, and unity.* It governs emotions like *empathy, forgiveness,* and the *desire for connection.* Today, we open our heart to this emerald-green energy allowing it to radiate from your chest. This is your endless fountain of love and compassion, and it's the mind of connection. ***Today is all about expanding your heart chakra and aligning with the universal rhythm of love and compassion.*** Turn on the Lion King soundtrack and let your mind swim across the great tundra. Here you are in the now, part animal, part spirit, mixing in the heart center so you can be alive on Earth. Let us hear you chant that sound out into the world.

"I LOVE"

The Embrace of Your Compassionate Heart

More than just love for others, the heart chakra is about cultivating unconditional love for yourself. ***"I love. I connect. I heal."*** These are the expressions of the heart chakra. It's about recognizing your inherent worthiness of love and embracing all aspects of yourself, including your flaws and imperfections.

This can be a challenge for many, especially those who have experienced heartbreak, rejection, or emotional wounds. ***We may build walls around our hearts, fearing vulnerability and intimacy.*** But the heart chakra reminds us that we are deserving of love, that we are connected to all beings, and that true healing comes from embracing our shared humanity.

"Anahata"

The name ***"Anahata"*** comes from Sanskrit and means "unhurt," "unstruck," or "unbeaten." This reflects the chakra's association with unconditional love, compassion, and spiritual healing. Our minds try to protect our hearts and build walls of protection but your heart is the entire piano of your experience and it loves to play all the notes. It is fearless in its ability to feel. When balanced, Anahata allows us to experience deep and meaningful connections, cultivate compassion for ourselves and others, and live with an open and loving heart. Heart Day is about embracing our true nature, which is inherently whole and unblemished, regardless of past experiences or external circumstances. ***Today we become mindful of the heart opening and closing. Then we learn to be brave enough to keep it open at all times.*** To understand the world, you need to feel it.

The Ego's Influence on Unconditional Love (Mind)

Remember that the ego can sometimes influence any chakra, including the heart chakra. When this happens, ***our capacity for love may become conditional***, dependent on external validation or the approval of others. *"I will love you as long as you love me."* Today that changes to, *"I am learning to love you all."* Today, ***we learn to give love away freely.*** We might find ourselves seeking love outside of ourselves or holding onto past hurts, which can block the flow of unconditional love, give it away freely and watch the world respond when it's time.

Instead of being led by the ego's tendencies, ***consider exploring your heart chakra from a place of self-acceptance and compassion, releasing judgment and this idea that there is a right and wrong in the world..*** You can cultivate unconditional love for yourself and others by ***embracing vulnerability and forgiveness.*** This opens your energy field to re-connect with the universal love that flows through all beings, allowing your heart to open and radiate compassion.

Healing Frequency – 639 Hz

The frequency 639 Hz is associated with the heart chakra to:

○   Promote Love and Connection: It helps to open the heart and enhance feelings of love, compassion, and connection.

○   Heal Relationships: This frequency is also associated with healing relationships and fostering harmony and balance.

○   Attract Love: 639 Hz can help to attract love and create deeper, more fulfilling relationships. Let the pure tones resonate through you all day.

BIJA MANTRA

"Yam"

"Yam" is the seed mantra or bija mantra associated with Anahata. Chanting "Yam" in 33 short repetitive sounds will open the chakra energy to:

○   **Activate and Balance the Chakra:** It vibrates within the chest, stimulating and harmonizing the energy of Anahata.

○   **Enhance Compassion:** It helps to cultivate compassion, empathy, and unconditional love.

○   **Promote Healing:** Chanting "Yam" in short repetition can help to heal emotional wounds and promote a sense of inner peace and harmony.

Divine Law Of The Universe (Soul)

Rhythm

———

Rhythm (Heart Chakra): The ego-mind often resists change, clinging to the illusion of permanence and control. The Law of Rhythm reveals the cyclical nature of life, with its ebb and flow, its periods of expansion and contraction. By connecting with the heart chakra and embracing the full spectrum of our emotions, we can learn to dance with life's rhythms, finding balance and acceptance amidst the ever-changing tides of existence. If our heart was a piano, we don't simply play the high notes, we play all the notes. Can you **resonate** with the rhythm of life. *Life is a dance of expansion and contraction. Learn to leave the heart open to the boundless love and compassion that reside within. Embrace the cyclical nature of life, finding balance and acceptance amidst the ever-changing rhythms of existence. The other part of rhythm is the structure of* **time**. *If we find ourselves to* **be impatient**, *sit with this chakra, because rhythm is also about* **learning how to trust divine timing.**

What is the Universal Law of Rhythm, and how is it associated with the heart?

What is the tone of your soul? What is the sound…your purest self makes? Can you sing your misery and can you sing your joy? Is this how you resonate with the universe…by making noise from within? The Universal Law of *Rhythm*, or the *Divine Concept* within the 4th Chakra, states that everything in the universe vibrates at a specific frequency, and we attract experiences and relationships that match our dominant vibration. The heart chakra, as our center of love and connection, plays a key role in this resonance process. *Today is about raising your frequency to match the life you want to co-create* with the world itself. Then, be in harmony with its flow.

The Law of Rhythm helps us by:

- **Attracting Love and Harmony:** The Law of Resonance teaches us that by cultivating love, compassion, and positive emotions, we can attract harmonious relationships and experiences into our lives. The heart chakra, when balanced, radiates a loving vibration that resonates with the universe, attracting positive energy and experiences.

- **Healing and Transformation:** The heart chakra is also associated with healing and transformation. By embracing forgiveness, compassion, and self-love, we can heal emotional wounds and create a more harmonious inner world. This, in turn, radiates outwards, influencing our relationships and the world around us. *The heart just needs permission to feel and it will handle the rest.*

Divine Guide - Bal'Thae'Zar (Ancestral)

The Emerald Dragon

From the verdant fields of the heart emerges Bal'Thae'Zar, the Angelic Emerald Dragon, a sacred being shimmering with the colors of new life. This gentle creature embodies the compassionate forces of love, empathy, and healing. With a loving embrace that soothes your soul, Bal'Thae'Zar awakens your connection to the heart chakra, reminding you of your innate capacity for unconditional love and connection. This dragon's love is gentle and nurturing, a soothing balm that heals emotional wounds and opens your heart to the beauty of the world.

Activity For The Day

1. Today's activities are all about remembering how to open your heart. We were all born into separation and we are all a little desperate for love, but that love does not need to come from external sources. You can generate endless love within your own being. For love to pour out, you learn how to remove the walls. Today you can spend all day in a mindful state of feeling how often your heart opens and closes. Bring a notebook and free-write when you feel the heart close, and then chant 'Yam' in quick succession and watch your heart open back up. *Let the music play*, learn to stand in the sad songs and the melodies of joy as the same. ***Feelings are the sound of your experience.*** You are the duality of light and shadow and your heart knows how to feel all of it, and it wants to, so we learn to set it free. ***"Quiet the mind, open the heart."*** Repeat until it you can feel it happen.

2. Go online or find a local gem store and acquire your favorite ***amethyst crystal***. Make sure it's a real deep purple and not a fake glass interpretation. This is your *"I love you crystal."* Carry it around with you all day today and whenever you see a person, in your mind, shoot them an "I love you". This energy is raising your frequency, lowering your mind of judgment, and loading that crystal with a source energy you can always access later during a healing meditation.

Yoga Practice

'Yoga Nidra' guides you through a powerful meditation practice to activate your heart chakra, fostering love, compassion, and inner peace within yourself that begins to radiate outwards. By combining breath work, visualization, and deep relaxation, you'll cultivate a more loving and open presence in your life.

Love without limits, that's the power of the heart. Break free from the chains of conditions, and let your compassion flow like a river, nourishing all it touches.

Anahata

CHAKRA ELEMENTS

639 hz   "I LOVE"   'Yam'

Gland/Body Part: Thymus Gland, Heart, Lungs, Circulatory System

Stones: Rose Quartz, Green Aventurine, Jade

Smells: Attar of Roses, Geranium

Colors: Emerald Green, Pink

Foods for Today: Leafy Greens, Vegetables, Fresh Fruits, Herbal Teas

Sacred Geometry: Circle with two intersecting triangles (Star of David) - Represents the union of opposites, and harmony between the physical and spiritual self.

Principle—Devotion, Self-Abandon

Element - Air

Rhythm

"I love. I connect. I heal."

Affirmation

"I release control of the mind—and feel the vibrations of my Soul."

Day 5
Throat Chakra

Vishuddha – "I Speak"

Your Words Are Magic.

Just wake up and hum. "Ham" as hummmm. Just lay there and hum over and over again until you feel the effortless flow of your vibrations mixing with the world. Feel the vibrations from your lower chakras pulse up into your throat as you release that energy out into the world. You can speak. You as sound. Activate this bright blue chakra and express yourself today by speaking with intention from your lower chakras. Speak from the heart, from your 2nd, speak from the root. Feel your ability to vibrate and speak as one. It's your voice, your truth, and your creative expression. Today, speak your truth clearly and honestly. The throat is the concept of turning your inner desires into vibrations that we call speech. You are co-creating from right here. Today, see your words as magic spells. When you speak, things happen. If you're afraid to speak, you are stuck. Speak from the abdomen, not the head. That is where your true essence spins with a willpower that is fearless and brave. Egoically, you want to speak for validation and gain, counter this by speaking from the heart, sending pulses of your true self out to the world. Today is not about letting your mind explain its stories, today we speak from the soul.

Your throat chakra is a beautiful, bright blue ball of spinning light, fiery and brave, ready to create. Picture this chakra like a projector: what you feed into this system will create your outer world. It's not just the words you use, but the frequency they carry. That is the true creator of this world—not the mind, but the vibrations from your soul. You were born to feel, and your feelings are the magic that shapes your reality.

"I SPEAK"

Expressing The Song Of Your Soul

We carry a deep desire to speak our truth, but one must first learn how to find their truth, in order to speak it."

More than just speaking, the throat chakra is about expressing the song of your soul. ***"I express. I am the magician. I can co-create with energy from within."*** So, "I speak" really means "I vibrate." You are the instrument, and you can create music. That is your song. To speak is not to be in service to the mind above but to learn how to let the identity from your abdomen travel up through your heart and out to the world without the need for fear tactics, worrying, or insecurity. ***When you speak from your lower chakras you create a powerful vibration of pure authenticity.***

This is often a struggle for both masculine and feminine energies. We've become accustomed to living in the mind, in a world of structure and logic, and we often express ourselves from this place. But true expression comes from the inner soul, the energy body that resonates from within. It arises from the depths of our being, processed through the second and third chakras (our centers of personal identity and willpower) and refined in the fourth chakra, the heart center.

The heart expresses upwards and outwards, carrying the wisdom of our soul. The mind, on the other hand, expresses downwards and outwards, often driven by narratives of survival and fear. The heart brings new data and intuitive wisdom, while the mind brings forth narratives and survival tactics. *Unleash the power of your voice, the magic of your words. Speak from the heart, with courage and compassion, and become a beacon of truth in a world yearning for authenticity.*

"Vishuddha"

The name *"Vishuddha"* comes from Sanskrit and means "especially pure" or "purification." This reflects the chakra's association with clear and truthful communication, free from distortions or negativity. It's about expressing yourself in a way that is aligned with your highest self and your authentic voice. Vishuddha, the fifth chakra, is located in the throat and is our center of expression, the bridge between our inner world and the outer world. As Yeshua wisely said, *"Make the inside like the outside,"* meaning that our inner truth should be reflected in our outer expression. This chakra governs communication, self-expression, and the ability to speak your truth. When balanced, *Vishuddha empowers you to communicate clearly, creatively, and with integrity. It allows you to express your thoughts, emotions, and ideas with authenticity and confidence.*

The Ego's Influence on Expression (Mind)

Remember that the ego can sometimes influence any chakra, including the heart chakra. When this happens, ***our capacity for love may become conditional***, dependent on external validation or the approval of others. *"I will love you as long as you love me."* Today that changes to, *"I am learning to love you all."* Today, ***we learn to give love away freely.*** We might find ourselves seeking love outside of ourselves or holding onto past hurts, which can block the flow of unconditional love, give it away freely and watch the world respond when it's time.

Instead of being led by the ego's tendencies, ***consider exploring your heart chakra from a place of self-acceptance and compassion, releasing judgment and this idea that there is a right and wrong in the world..*** You can cultivate unconditional love for yourself and others by ***embracing vulnerability and forgiveness.*** This opens your energy field to re-connect with the universal love that flows through all beings, allowing your heart to open and radiate compassion.

SOUND & FREQUENCY (Body)

Healing Frequency – 741 Hz

The frequency 741 Hz is associated with the throat chakra to promote:

o   **Expression and Problem Solving:** This frequency can enhance communication skills, helping you articulate your thoughts and feelings clearly and effectively.

o   **Purification and Cleansing:** This frequency is also associated with cleansing the energy field and promoting a sense of clarity and purity within the throat chakra, allowing for clear and honest expression.

o   **Intuition and Inspiration:** 741 Hz can stimulate intuition and inspire creative expression, helping you tap into your inner wisdom and share it with the world.

BIJA MANTRA

"Ham"

"Ham" is the seed mantra or bija mantra associated with Vishuddha. Chanting "Ham" (Haum) in 33 short repetitive sounds will open the chakra energy to:

- **Activate and Balance the Chakra:** It vibrates within the throat area, stimulating and harmonizing the energy of Vishuddha.

- **Enhance Communication:** It helps to clear blockages that hinder self-expression and promotes clear, authentic communication.

- **Connect to Truth:** Chanting "Ham" can help you connect to your inner truth and express it with confidence and clarity.

Divine Law Of The Universe (Soul)

VIBRATION

Vibration (Throat Chakra): The ego often blocks authentic self-expression in the 3rd chakra, leading to inauthentic communication and a diminished sense of personal power. The Law of Vibration reminds us that everything is in constant motion, vibrating at a specific frequency . By aligning with the throat chakra and expressing our truth with courage and clarity, we can raise our vibration and attract experiences that resonate with our authentic selves. *Everything in the universe is in constant motion, vibrating at a specific frequency. Express your authentic voice through your throat chakra. Recognize that everything is energy in motion, and by speaking your truth from the heart instead of the mind, you can create a ripple effect of authenticity in the world.*

What is the Universal Law of Vibration, and how is it associated with the throat?

The *Universal Law of Vibration*, or the *Divine Concept* within the 5th Chakra, states that everything in the universe is in a constant state of motion, vibrating at a specific frequency. This includes our thoughts, emotions, words, and actions. Each vibration carries a unique energy signature. So ask yourself, *how much do you block this energy? How much of your authentic expressions is blocked by the tactics of our mind?*

o   **Expression and Manifestation:** The Law of Vibration teaches us that by becoming aware of and aligning our vibrations with our deeper intentions, we can manifest our soul desires and create positive change. The throat chakra, as the center of physical expression, plays a key role in co-creating our reality.

o   **Authenticity and Harmony:** When we express ourselves authentically, our communication becomes more powerful and impactful. We can inspire, uplift, and create positive change through our words and actions. This is learning to speak without mental attachments or a wounded need for validation. Are you speaking, or is your wound? Are you communicating, or is your mind? To be authentic is to speak without needs or wants; it's to speak out of love. The throat chakra, when balanced, allows our true voice to shine through, resonating with our authentic vibration.

<h1 style="text-align:center">Divine Guide - E'Ok 'N (Ayok-un) (Ancestral)</h1>

<h2 style="text-align:center">The Blue Dragon</h2>

From the clear sky of your soul emerges E'Ok'N, the Blue Dragon, its scales shimmering like sunlight on water. This wise creature embodies the expressive power of communication, truth, and authenticity. With a loving song that resonates through your being, E'Ok'N awakens your connection to the throat chakra, reminding you of your innate ability to speak your truth and inspire others with your voice. This dragon's love is clear and unwavering, a beacon of light that guides you towards expressing the unique melody of your soul.

Honest Communication

Honest communication comes from the ability to be openly flawed and openly beautiful, just as you are. Think about how much you don't say, the relentless narrator of your mind saying things we dare not repeat. That is the mind trying to control itself, to edit and censor your true expression. The heart-mind is different. Speaking from the heart is pure authenticity. It is you, naked from the inside, fearless to show the world who you really are. To truly learn to speak, we learn to be honest from the core of our soul. There is no good or bad, no right or wrong, in this space of authentic expression. That is the trick the mind plays on us. You cannot control your true expression; you have to let that energy move through you without judgment, without control, without shame or guilt.

The Koshas and the Throat Chakra

The ancient yogic concept of the Koshas offers a powerful lens through which to examine the motivations behind your communication. These five sheaths, or layers, represent different aspects of your being:. Here are the first three that relate to our journey from head to heart awakening:

- **Annamaya Kosha (Physical Body):** This is the most tangible layer, encompassing your physical form, senses, and primal instincts. Desires originating here are often linked to survival, pleasure, and comfort.

- **Pranamaya Kosha (Energy Body):** This layer governs your life force energy (Prana), which flows through your chakras and subtle channels. Desires arising here are often linked to your soul's purpose and spiritual growth.

- **Manomaya Kosha (Mental Body):** This layer encompasses your thoughts, emotions, and beliefs. Desires stemming from this layer are often shaped by your past experiences, conditioning, and ego-driven needs.

Now assign each of your desires to a Kosha. When you communicate, ask yourself: Which Kosha is motivating my expression? Is it the physical desire for safety or approval? Is it the soul's yearning to connect and share its truth? Or is it the mind's need to control, manipulate, or defend? By understanding the Koshas, you can become more aware of the underlying motivations behind your communication and make conscious choices about how you express yourself. If your words are magic, then ***knowing what is driving you to speak will be the source that changes your reality.***

Yoga Pose

Fish Pose (Matsyasana) — Open your throat and release any blockages to self-expression.

Your truth is your power. Speak it with the unwavering authority of your heart, and let your voice rise above the noise, igniting a fearless symphony of authentic expression.

Vishuddha
CHAKRA ELEMENTS
741 hz   "I SPEAK"   'Ham'
Gland/Body Part: Thyroid Gland, Throat, Neck, Mouth, Ears
Stones: Turquoise, Aquamarine, Lapis Lazuli, Blue Lace Agate
Smells: Eucalyptus, Peppermint, Chamomile
Colors: Cyan Blue, Turquoise
Foods for Today: Liquids, Fruits, Herbal Tea
Sacred Geometry: Downward-pointing triangle within a circle - Represents purification and the decent of divine energy into the physical world
Principle—Resonance Of Being
Element - Ether
Vibration

"I feel, I belong, I speak from my soul"

Affirmation

"I release the limitations of self. I open my mind to the Universe."

3rd Eye Chakra

Ajna – "I See"

Beyond The Self.

Rest the palm of your hand on your forehead, and the palm of your other hand on the back of your head. You are holding something very powerful. Ajna, the sixth chakra, resides in the center of your forehead, projecting between your eyebrows, glowing with a beautiful indigo hue. If you can see the world in front of you with your eyes, then you can see the bigger picture through your spiritual eye. Your third eye indeed. The 3rd eye is the WIFI of the masters, the key to unlocking your potential to commune with your divine and become *a conscious* co-creator of your reality. ***When balanced, Ajna empowers you to perceive the world with clarity, to trust your inner wisdom, and to access higher states of consciousness.*** It allows you *to see the interconnectedness of all things* and *to understand the deeper meaning and purpose of your life.*

This radiant Ajna energy embodies *wisdom, awakening, and clairvoyance*—it's about openness, understanding, and a little soul magic. It becomes blocked in a state of needing to be right or believing we know something we only understand intellectually. To know is to feel, not to think. But this masterful chakra challenges us by asking, *"Can you close your eyes and see the truth?"* This is the awakening of your higher mind. This chakra has a vision that extends beyond the physical. Your 'quantum eye' if you will. *Ajna allows you to perceive the world with greater clarity and insight, to tap into your inner wisdom, and to awaken to your higher intellect.*

"I SEE"

Beyond The Self

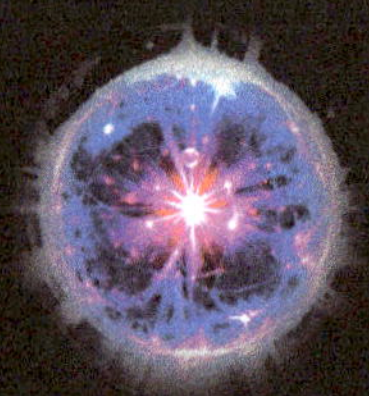

Ajna allows you *to see beyond the limitations of your individual self,* to perceive the interconnectedness of all beings and the subtle energies that weave through the universe. But what does "I see" truly mean in the context of the third eye? It's not just about visualizing images or having psychic visions. It's about a deeper understanding, an awareness that transcends the limitations of our physical senses and our individual ego. Perhaps *"I see"* signifies a knowing, a comprehension that goes beyond visual perception. It's the ability to grasp the interconnectedness of all things, to perceive the underlying unity beneath the surface of appearances. *It's about recognizing the divine spark within yourself and all beings.* It's about seeing with the eyes of your soul, with the eyes of the collective consciousness. *True wisdom and healing come from integrating the intellect with the intuition, the rational with the emotional.*

"Ajna"

The name **"Ajna"** comes from Sanskrit and means **"command"** or **"perceive."** This reflects the chakra's association with clear seeing, intuition, and wisdom. It's about perceiving the world and yourself with clarity and insight, free from the distortions of the ego and the limitations of the five senses. Ajna, the sixth chakra, is located in the center of the forehead, between the eyebrows. It is considered the center of intuition, wisdom, and spiritual vision. It acts as a bridge between the physical and spiritual worlds, allowing you to access deeper levels of consciousness and connect with your inner guidance. Have a very purply divine third-eye day.

The Ego's Influence on Intuition (Mind)

The Ego is the mind of Self. Remember that the ego can sometimes cloud the clarity of any chakra, including the third eye. When this happens, our intuition may become distorted by the ego's needs for control, validation, and the illusion of knowledge. We might find ourselves resisting intuitive nudges that challenge our beliefs or lead us outside our comfort zones. We might overanalyze and doubt our inner wisdom, seeking external validation instead of trusting our inner guidance.

Instead of being led by the ego's tendencies, consider exploring your third eye chakra from a place of openness and surrender. Quiet the mind, release the need to be right, and allow space for intuitive whispers to emerge. You could cultivate a deep connection with your inner wisdom, allowing yourself to be guided by the subtle nudges and insights that arise from within. Embrace the unknown with curiosity and a willingness to see beyond the limitations of your current understanding.

Healing Frequency – 852 Hz

The frequency 852 Hz is associated with the 3rd eye chakra to promote:

o   **Enhance Connection:** It strengthens your connection to your higher self and the subtle realms.

o   **Promote Clarity:** It helps to clear mental fog and enhance your ability to focus and perceive clearly.

o   **Connect to the Spiritual:** It facilitates a deeper connection to your spiritual self and the unseen realms.

BIJA MANTRA

"Om"

"Om" is the seed mantra associated with Ajna. *It's considered the primordial sound of creation,* the vibration that resonates throughout the universe. In many spiritual traditions, "Om" represents the divine, the ultimate reality, the source of all that is. It's the sound that connects us to the universal consciousness. In a near death experience one man even described God as this, *"Well, it felt more like a woman, and matter of fact, it wasn't really a person at all, it was this divine energy, and it sounded like, Om."*

"Om" is the seed mantra or bija mantra associated with Vishuddha.
Chanting "Om" in 33 short repetitive sounds will open the chakra energy to:

o   **Activate the Third Eye:** It stimulates and balances the energy of Ajna, opening your channels of communication.

o   **Enhance Connection:** It deepens your connection to your inner guidance and the divine.

o   **Expand Consciousness:** It helps to expand your awareness beyond the limitations of the physical world.

Divine Law Of The Universe (Soul)

CORRESPONDANCE

Correspondence (Third Eye Chakra): The ego often distorts our perception of reality, leading us to believe that our inner and outer worlds are separate. The Law of Correspondence, "as above, so below, so within as without." challenges our belief of separation by highlighting the interconnectedness between our inner state and our external experiences. By activating the third eye chakra and developing our intuition, we can see beyond the ego's illusions and perceive the world with greater clarity and understanding. To send and receive. This is about recognizing the duality of our minds – the outward-facing mind of the ego and the inward-facing mind connected to the source. A reminder that we can choose our mind of self or the mind of all that is.

What is the Universal Law of Correspondence, and how is it associated with the 3rd eye?

Correspondence means to "command" or "perceive." To perceive the unseen and to direct your life with clarity and purpose through clear communication with your inner self and the universe. But notice how it reveals some deeper truths, it moves in two directions. To command or to perceive. This chakra reminds us that *Communication* is not just about words, but about *an energetic exchange between beings.* When opened, *this is your channel for receiving guidance and inspiration, which can lead to profound understanding.* This requires a state of being free from the ego, free from the distortions of judgment and the skewed thinking of our wounds. *It allows for pure translation, pure communication from the higher self, unmanipulated by the mind.* The trick is trying to surrender to your mind of self and allow your higher mind to see the world with more clarity.

Ajna, as the center of subtle communication, allows you to:

o   **Connect with your Higher Self:** Engage in a dialogue with your soul, your inner wisdom, and the deeper aspects of your being.

o   **Communicate with the Divine:** Open a channel to the divine, to guides, angels, and ascended masters.

o   **Receive Guidance and Inspiration:** Tune into the subtle whispers of the universe, receiving insights, messages, and inspiration.

o   **Transmit Your Intentions:** Project your thoughts, desires, and intentions out into the world influencing the manifestation of your reality.

The Indigo Dragon

From the depths of the cosmic spine emerges Cy'thwaete, the Indigo Goddess who embodies the celestial 3rd-Eye Chakra, its energy body shimmering with the waterfall of the universe. This mystical creature embodies the intuitive wisdom of water and the portals of the third-eye, guiding you towards deeper understanding and connection with the divine. With a loving gaze that pierces through illusion, Cy'thwaete awakens your inner vision, revealing the hidden truths and subtle energies that surround you. This dragon's love is wise and insightful, a beacon of clarity that illuminates your path towards spiritual awakening.

'We are a river of consciousness. I flow the waters of the heavens down to you, to nourish you. I am closely related to spiritual vision but I am also close to the other senses. The Clairs. I am like an artery from the heart of the cosmos. I come from the angelic realms and that is where I live. Together, you and I are creating a gateway between heaven and Earth. Many of you have busy minds like a turbulent storm. I encourage you to find the stillness in your mind. I will open an energy channel between you and the cosmic heavens if you choose to accept."

Activity For The Day

What does it mean to see? It means we leave the mind of self and expand into a higher awareness, higher on the mountain where now we look back and exclaim, ***"Oh, now I can truly see."*** We see with our lower minds and our higher minds and today is all about learning to switch between the two. This breathing technique is ancient in its roots and blooms in the now. A powerful and delicate technique to open your *higher mind.*

This technique uses a specific pattern of nasal breathing to activate the flow of prana, awaken the pineal gland and crown chakra, and cultivate a deeper connection to your Spirit Mind.

1. **Right Nostril Breathing:** Begin by gently closing your left nostril with your right hand. Inhale slowly and deeply through your right nostril, visualizing the breath flowing up into the **nasopharynx** (the upper part of the pharynx, connecting the nasal cavity to the throat). Feel the solar energy activating and warming the body.

2. **Left Nostril Breathing:** Release your right hand and gently close your right nostril with your left hand. Inhale slowly and deeply through your left nostril, visualizing the breath flowing up into the nasopharynx. Feel the lunar energy cooling and calming the body.

3. **Unified Breathing:** Release both nostrils and inhale deeply through both, visualizing the breath flowing up into the nasopharynx. As you inhale, become aware of the cooling sensation behind the eyes, a sign of nitric oxide engaging with the pineal gland. Gently draw this cooling energy to the center of your mind, activating your third eye. Then, focus your attention on the pineal gland, the seat of your intuition and inner vision.

4. **Crown Activation:** Continue breathing deeply through both nostrils, holding your awareness at the pineal gland. As you breathe, visualize a warm, golden light expanding from the pineal gland to the crown of your head. Feel the crown chakra opening, allowing a gentle flow of source energy to drip into your mind like honey, filling you with a sense of peace and expanded awareness.

Tips and Tricks

o   Find a comfortable seated position with your spine straight.

o   Keep your breath slow, smooth, and gentle throughout the practice.

o   You can incorporate a gentle breath retention (holding the breath for a few seconds) after each inhalation if it feels comfortable.

o   If you experience any discomfort or dizziness, gently release the practice and return to normal breathing.

o   Practice this technique regularly to cultivate a deeper connection to your Spirit Mind and enhance your intuition, creativity, and spiritual awareness.

Yoga Pose

***Child's Pose (Balasana)** . Calm the mind to awaken your higher self in complete surrender.*

As you clear away the dust and awaken this powerful energy center, you'll begin to perceive the world with new clarity. It's a gateway to deeper understanding, to the unseen realms of wisdom and guidance.

Ajna

CHAKRA ELEMENTS

852 hz   "I SEE"   'Om'

Gland/Body Part: Pituitary Gland, Pineal Gland, Eyes, Head

Stones: Amethyst, Sodalite, Clear Quartz

Smells: Lavender, Frankincense, Sandalwood

Colors: Indigo, Purple, Violet

Foods for Today: Dark-colored Fruits & Vegetables, Raw Foods, Juices

Sacred Geometry: Two intersecting triangles
Represents the union of intuition and intellect, and the balance between the physical and spiritual worlds.

Principle—Knowledge Of Being

Element - Light

Correspondence

"I see beyond the self"

Affirmation

"I release the mind of limitation and surround myself with light."

Day 7
Crown Chakra

Sahasrara – "I Understand"

Your Connection To The Divine

Rest your hands gently on the crown of your head. Feel the subtle pulsation of energy, a gentle thrumming that connects you to the vastness of the cosmos. Sahasrara, the seventh chakra, resides at the top of your head, a radiant vortex of violet light, often visualized as a radiant star or a luminous orb. If your physical eyes allow you to perceive the world around you, then *your crown chakra opens you to the boundless expanse of the universe, the spiritual realms, and the divine source of all creation.*

This is the chakra of enlightenment, of transcendence, of unity with all that is. *It's about opening to the infinite wisdom and unconditional love that permeate the cosmos.* When balanced, Sahasrara empowers you to experience a deep sense of peace, purpose, and connection to something greater than yourself. It allows you to access higher states of consciousness, to recognize your inherent divinity, and to live in harmony with the universal flow. This radiant Sahasrara energy embodies enlightenment, spiritual connection, and divine wisdom. It's about surrendering to the greater wisdom of the universe and trusting in the unfolding of your soul's journey. It becomes blocked when we cling to the illusion of separation, when we limit ourselves with fear and doubt. Your crown chakra invites us to ask, *"Can I surrender to the unknown and embrace the infinite possibilities that lie beyond my perceived limitations?"*

This is the awakening of your spiritual heart, your connection to the divine essence that permeates all beings. This chakra has a vision that extends beyond the confines of the individual self, *allowing you to perceive the interconnectedness of all life* and to experience the profound unity that underlies the apparent diversity of the universe. Sahasrara allows you to perceive the world with expanded awareness, to tap into the universal wisdom, and to awaken to your true nature as a spiritual being.

"I UNDERSTAND"

The Self & The Soul

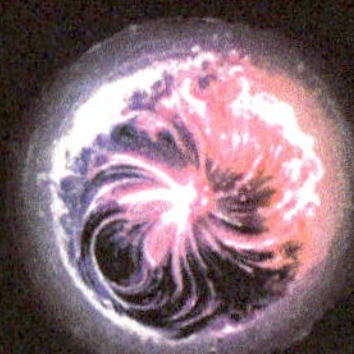

More than just spiritual connection, the crown chakra is about accessing the wisdom of your soul mind. *"I understand. I transcend. I am one with all."* These are the realizations of the crown chakra. It's about recognizing your interconnectedness with all beings and experiencing a profound sense of unity with the universe. We understand because instead of thinking, we are listening. This can be a challenge for many, especially those who are deeply rooted in the material world or who have experienced spiritual disconnection. We may feel lost, alone, or disconnected from our spiritual essence. But **the crown chakra reminds us that we are part of something larger than ourselves, that we are connected to the divine, and that we have the potential to access higher states of consciousness.**

Sitting Meditation with a Crown Chakra Mudra: Even a simple seated meditation can be enhanced by incorporating a mudra (hand gesture) that activates the crown chakra. One common mudra is to gently touch the tips of the thumb and index finger together, with the other three fingers extended straight. Exhale, resting the hands palms-up on the knees. *(Gyan Mudra)* This mudra is connecting you with wisdom and knowledge.

"Sahasrara"

The name **"Sahasrara"** comes from Sanskrit and means **"thousand-petaled."** *This reflects the chakra's association with **infinite potential, enlightenment, and the transcendence of limitations.*** It's about perceiving yourself and the world through the lens of unity, recognizing the divine spark within all beings and experiencing the boundless love and wisdom that connect us all. Sahasrara, the seventh chakra, acts as a gateway to the divine, allowing you to access higher states of consciousness and experience the fullness of your being. Have a divinely violet crown chakra day.

<h2 style="text-align:center">The Ego's Influence on Spiritual Connection (Mind)</h2>

The Ego is the mind of Self. Remember that the ego can sometimes influence any chakra, including the crown chakra. When this happens, *our spiritual pursuits may become distorted by the ego's need for control, validation, and separation. We might find ourselves seeking spiritual experiences to boost our ego or to escape from reality, which can hinder our true spiritual growth.*

Instead of being led by the ego's tendencies, *consider exploring your crown chakra from a place of humility and surrender.* You could cultivate a deep connection, allowing yourself to be guided by a higher power. You could embrace the unknown with an open heart and mind, trusting in the wisdom of the universe.

<h2 style="text-align:center">SOUND & FREQUENCY (Body)</h2>

Healing Frequency – 963 Hz

The frequency 963 Hz is associated with the Sahasrara chakra to promote:

o   **Promote Spiritual Connection:** It helps to activate the crown chakra and enhance your connection to the divine.

o   **Awaken Higher Consciousness:** This frequency is also associated with awakening higher states of consciousness and accessing spiritual enlightenment.

o   **Facilitate Oneness:** Some believe 963 Hz can help to experience a sense of oneness and unity with the universe.

BIJA MANTRA

"Aum"

Why is the mantra Aum instead of Om?

OM is the seed sound of the third eye chakra (Ajna), representing unity, intuition, and connection to the divine. It's a single, continuous sound that resonates with the essence of oneness and unconditional love. AUM, on the other hand, is the seed sound of the crown chakra (Sahasrara). It's chanted with three distinct sounds – A, U, and M – creating a cycle of energy that mirrors the continuous flow of creation and the interconnectedness of all things.

Imagine AUM as a swirling vortex of energy, drawing you upwards towards the crown of your being, connecting you to the source of all creation. The three sounds resonate with different aspects of the cosmos:

- o **A: Represents the beginning, the creation, the expansion of consciousness.**
- o **U: Represents the preservation, the sustenance, the balance of energy.**
- o **M: Represents the dissolution, the transformation, the return to source.**

Together, these three sounds create a complete cycle, a continuous flow of energy that reflects the dynamic nature of the universe. So, while OM connects you to the unity of the third eye, AUM activates the dynamic flow of energy through the crown chakra, opening you to the boundless expanse of the cosmos and the infinite potential within.

MENTALISM

Mentalism (Crown Chakra): The Law of Mentalism reminds us that we are not just isolated individuals but interconnected beings, part of a vast universal consciousness. When we say, "All is mind" what we mean is, "all is thought." Your curios soul is creating a world with all of us too. Our thoughts effect energy and we create life. Thoughts are the instructions and energy is what we use to build. Thought and energy—structure and chaos—defined and undefined—masculine feminine. This is the root of our entire duality. By quieting the ego-mind and connecting with the crown chakra, we can access this universal mind, the soul, reattaching us to a more pure form of thought, which we refer to as our "higher mind." It's not higher, it's simply less egoic. This is the place where thought and energy merge to create our existence.

What is the Universal Law of Mentalism, and how is it associated with the Crown Chakra?

Mentalism (Crown Chakra): The ego-mind, with its focus on the individual self, often creates a sense of separation from the divine, a feeling of limitation and lack. The Law of Mentalism reminds us that we are not just isolated individuals but interconnected beings, part of a vast universal consciousness . By quieting the ego-mind and connecting with the crown chakra, we can access this universal mind, the soul, realizing our true potential and experiencing a profound sense of unity with all of creation. This is about recognizing the duality of our minds – the outward-facing mind of the ego and the inward-facing mind connected to the source. A reminder that we can choose our mind of self or the mind of all that is. A place where thought and energy merge to create our existence.

The universe is a mental creation, a divine curiosity, and your curiosities shape your reality. This law, is about more than just the "mind" as we typically understand it. It's about "I Understand," a deep inner knowing, a connection to something bigger than ourselves, a transcendence of the limitations of the ego-self. By connecting with this chakra, we tap into the boundless wisdom of the universal mind, experiencing a sense of unity and interconnectedness with all that is.

Divine Guide - *Flec'An'Da'Cian* (Ancestral)

The White Dragon

From the celestial realms descends *Flec'An'Da'Cian*, the White Dragon, its scales shimmering with the colors of the cosmos. She embodies a peace we have all forgotten and long to feel. When she is present your body resonates with a state of calm, a state of safety, and a state of divine wisdom and grace. This ethereal creature embodies the divine connection of the crown chakra, guiding you towards spiritual awakening and unity consciousness. With a loving embrace that transcends the boundaries of the physical world, Flec'An'Da'Cian awakens your connection to the divine heavens, reminding you of your infinite potential and your inherent oneness with all beings. That she is you and you are her. The white dragon's love is unconditional and boundless, a gateway to experiencing the divine serenity within and all around you.

"I am a white dragon of peace. I bring peace to the base of who you are. Accept the conflict for what it is entirely and make peace with what is. We see that all of you can do no wrong, for you went into the seasons of winter, like a seed that felt the sorrow of feeling disconnected. Now you are awakening and we will reconnect. I am here to bring the energy of peace into your being."

The Path To Unconditional Love

*The Soul Chakra **holds 0 parts conditional and 7 parts unconditional.** We have traveled from the darkness to the light, from one magnetic pole to the other. Our journey to unfold followed the geometric expansion from conditional love (structure and limitation) to unconditional love (transcendence of the conditional world of limitation.) When we awaken both dual aspects of who we are we can then learn to harmonize all facets of our being, light, shadow, ancestral, and the now. As we walked the path from separation, we unified our own being while re-connecting to all that is. Not knowing who we are can cause us to split into a million pieces. When we align with who we are, which is a unity consciousness created by all beings, we find ourselves once again. To become whole is to transcend the self to remember you are two parts, a conditional experience driven by an unconditional soul. **All parts unconditional love. Does this mean we have transcended conditions?** No, it means we have studied our conditions and become them. The geometry of the soul is an expansion of the place we started on the x and y axis. To understand this shape we have become all the shapes within it. We are unconditional, not because we are free of conditions, but because we understand them deeply.*

Yoga Pose

Sitting Meditation with a Crown Chakra Mudra: Even a simple seated meditation can be enhanced by incorporating a mudra (hand gesture) that activates the crown chakra. One common mudra is to gently touch the tips of the thumb and index finger together, with the other three fingers extended straight. Exhale, resting the hands palms-up on the knees. *(Gyan Mudra)* This mudra is connecting you with wisdom and knowledge.

Activity For The Day

Reiki Golden Ball Meditation

This meditation invites you to connect with the healing energy of Reiki and visualize a golden ball of light to activate and balance your chakras, culminating in a profound opening of the crown chakra:

1. **Preparation:** Find a comfortable seated or lying down position. Close your eyes and take a few deep breaths to relax your body and mind.

2. **Inviting Reiki:** If you've been attuned to Reiki, you can draw the Reiki symbols in the air or visualize them in your mind's eye. Even if you haven't been attuned, you can simply invite the healing energy of Reiki to flow through you.

3. **Golden Ball Visualization:** Visualize a radiant golden ball of light hovering above your head. See it pulsating with vibrant energy and feel its warmth and love.

4. **Chakra Journey:** Gently guide the golden ball down through your energy centers, starting with the crown chakra. As it passes through each chakra, visualize it cleansing and balancing the energy, removing any blockages and restoring harmony.

5. **Crown Chakra Activation:** When the golden ball reaches your crown chakra, allow it to linger there, expanding and filling your entire being with its radiant light. Feel a sense of deep connection to the divine, a sense of oneness with all creation.

6. **Integration:** Allow the golden ball to slowly dissolve into your crown chakra, leaving you feeling revitalized, balanced, and connected to your higher self.

7. **Journaling:** After the meditation, take some time to journal about your experience. What sensations did you notice? What insights or emotions arose? How did the energy of the golden ball affect each chakra?

This meditation is a powerful tool for self-healing and spiritual growth. It can be practiced regularly to cultivate a deeper connection and enhance your overall well-being.

"I am open, I am free, I am one with all."

And So It Begins,

The sun sets on our seven-day journey, and we stand transformed, not just with knowledge, but with a visceral awareness of our own energy body. It's no longer an esoteric concept, but a tangible reality, a vibrant landscape of spinning wheels of light – our chakras. We've moved beyond the intellectual and into the experiential, feeling the truth of these ancient pathways in every cell.

This is the awakening. It's not just about *knowing* the chakras, but about *being* them, embodying their essence in our everyday lives. We've felt the root's grounding force, anchoring us to the Earth, securing us in our existence. We've unleashed the sacral's creative fire, embracing the dance of passion and pleasure that fuels our manifestations. We've ignited the solar plexus, our core of personal power, claiming our authentic selves and becoming accountable for our desires. We've opened our hearts to the boundless love of Anahata, healing old wounds and radiating compassion outwards. We've found our voice in Vishuddha, a clear channel for authentic expression, vibrating with the truth of our soul. We've peered through the third eye, glimpsing the subtle energies that weave the creation of our reality. And we've touched the crown of our being, Sahasrara, bathed in the serenity of divine connection.

This illuminous pathway colors our perceptions, shape our experiences, and guide us toward growth and understanding. They are the teachers who never tire, the healers who mend our fragmented selves, the guides who lead us back to wholeness.

This journey through the chakras is a journey through the mind, body, and soul, through the very essence of who we are and how we manifest in physical reality. It's a journey of remembering, of reclaiming the innate wisdom that resides within. And as we carry this wisdom forward, we step into our power as conscious creators, shaping our reality with intention, with awareness, and with the unwavering remembrance of our true, luminous selves. Your chakras hold the map to your soul's unfolding; let their wisdom guide you home to the love you were always meant to be. The great remembering begins. *We are souls in bodies. Go. Be.*

If you're deeply resonating with your chakras, there is oh so much more, and they are all divine indeed. Above the crown exists your realm of higher chakras, each a gateway to greater spiritual awareness, universal wisdom, and divine love.

As you travel out of your body you have plenty of stops along the way. Most of us resonate with one of these sacred chakras and often see their characteristics playing out in our lives. As we expand up from our crown chakra, the Five of Light expand us further and further into the realms of the Gods.

o   **8th Chakra: Soul Star -** (Pale Silver) – In Sanskrit, *'Terra (star) Chakra'* connects you to your soul's blueprint and divine purpose. *Feeling lost or lacking direction?* This chakra illuminates your path and guides you towards your highest destiny.

o   **9th Chakra: Universal Heart** (Gold) - In Sanskrit the *Hridaya (cosmic heart) Chakra* expands your capacity for compassion and connects you to the universal heart. *Feeling isolated?* This chakra opens you to the boundless love that permeates all creation.

o   **10th Chakra: Divine Gateway** (Diamond White) - The *Divya (heavenly) Dwar (door) Chakra* opens a portal to higher realms and communication with spirit guides and ascended masters. *Feeling disconnected from spiritual guidance?* This chakra opens the doorway to divine wisdom and support.

- o **11th Chakra: Causal** (Iridescent) - Do you see 11's everywhere? Curious indeed. The ***Karan (causal) Chakra*** holds the keys to your soul's journey through time, revealing past-life memories and karmic patterns. *Karan* means "cause" or "origin," referring to the causal plane of existence where the soul's journey and karmic patterns originate. ***Feeling stuck in repetitive cycles?*** This chakra offers profound insights and the potential for liberation.

- o **12th Chakra: Stellar Gateway** (Deep Magenta) – The ***Brahmarandhra Chakra*** connects to the cosmos and your place in the universe. *Brahmarandhra* translates to "the doorway to Heaven," signifying the point of connection between the individual consciousness and the universal consciousness. ***Feeling lost in the vastness?*** This chakra anchors you to the stars and reveals your unique role in the cosmic dance.

As we ascend through these higher chakras, we begin to unravel the layers of our restricted minds, opening to a vast expanse of cosmic awareness. We connect with our soul family, the universe, and the divine essence that unites us all. The journey of awakening is infinite, and the 5 of Light offer a glimpse into the boundless potential that awaits us. Enjoy the journey and love the transformation.

And if you are still wondering what all of this means, the *why* we are here.

To love. *Love is why we are here.*

"I AM"

The Seed of Existence

The Elements

Muladhara

CHAKRA ELEMENTS

396hz   "I AM"   'Lam'

Gland/Body Part: Adrenal glands, base of the spine, legs, feet, bones.

Stones: Red jasper, black tourmaline, hematite, garnet

Smells: Cedarwood, patchouli, myrrh

Colors: Red, black, brown

Foods for Today: Root vegetables, protein-rich foods

Sacred Geometry: Downward-pointing triangle: Symbolizes the Earth element and connection to the physical world.

Principle—Stability and Security

Element - Earth

Gender/Generation

Svadhisthana

CHAKRA ELEMENTS

417 hz   **"I FEEL"**   **'Vam'**

Gland/Body Part: Gonads (ovaries/testes), lower abdomen, kidneys, bladder

Stones: Carnelian, Moonstone, Orange Calcite

Smells: Ylang-Ylang, Sandalwood, Citrus

Colors: Orange, Peach, Terracotta

Foods for Today: Fruits, Nuts, Seeds, Chocolate

Sacred Geometry: The Crescent Moon shape is the connection to lunar energy, emotions, and the subconscious

Principle— Creative Reproduction Of Being

Element - Water

Polarity

Manipura

CHAKRA ELEMENTS

528 hz   "I DO"   'Ram'

Gland/Body Part: Pancreas, Digestive System, Liver, Gallbladder

Stones: Citrine, Tiger's Eye, Amber, Yellow Jasper

Smells: Lemon, Rosemary, Peppermint

Colors: Yellow, Gold

Foods for Today: Grains, Yellow Fruits & Vegetables, Complex Carbohydrates

Sacred Geometry: Inverted Triangle - Represents the ability to harness and direct energy at will.

Principle—Shaping Of Your Being

Element - Fire

Cause & Effect

Anahata

CHAKRA ELEMENTS

639 hz   "I LOVE"   'Yam'

Gland/Body Part: Thymus Gland, Heart, Lungs, Circulatory System

Stones: Rose Quartz, Green Aventurine, Jade

Smells: Attar of Roses, Geranium

Colors: Emerald Green, Pink

Foods for Today: Leafy Greens, Vegetables, Fresh Fruits, Herbal Teas

Sacred Geometry: Circle with two intersecting triangles (Star of David) - Represents the union of opposites, and harmony between the physical and spiritual self.

Principle—Devotion, Self-Abandon

Element - Air

Rhythm

Vishuddha

CHAKRA ELEMENTS

741 hz   "I SPEAK"   'Ham'

Gland/Body Part: Thyroid Gland, Throat, Neck, Mouth, Ears

Stones: Turquoise, Aquamarine, Lapis Lazuli, Blue Lace Agate

Smells: Eucalyptus, Peppermint, Chamomile

Colors: Cyan Blue, Turquoise

Foods for Today: Liquids, Fruits, Herbal Tea

Sacred Geometry: Downward-pointing triangle within a circle - Represents purification and the decent of divine energy into the physical world

Principle—Resonance Of Being

Element - Ether

Vibration

Ajna

CHAKRA ELEMENTS

852 hz   **"I SEE"**   **'Om'**

Gland/Body Part: Pituitary Gland, Pineal Gland, Eyes, Head

Stones: Amethyst, Sodalite, Clear Quartz

Smells: Lavender, Frankincense, Sandalwood

Colors: Indigo, Purple, Violet

Foods for Today: Dark-colored Fruits & Vegetables, Raw Foods, Juices

Sacred Geometry: Two intersecting triangles
Represents the union of intuition and intellect, and the balance between the physical and spiritual worlds.

Principle—Knowledge Of Being

Element - Light

Correspondence

Sahasrara

CHAKRA ELEMENTS

963 hz   "I UNDERSTAND"   'AUM'

Gland/Body Part: Pineal Gland, Central Nervous System, Brain

Stones: Amethyst, Sodalite, Clear Quartz

Smells: Lavender, Frankincense, Myrh

Colors: Violet, White, Gold, Silver

Foods for Today: Fasting, Light and Pure foods, Spiritual Practices

Sacred Geometry: The Circle - Represents Unity, Wholeness, and Connction to the Divine.

Principle — Connection

Element - Conciousness

Mentalism/Thought